John Wieners
Solitary Pleasure

Selected Poetry, Journals
and Ephemera

Pilot Press
London

Selected Poems

The Asylum Poems

Miscellaneous Journal Entries and Ephemera

Types of solitariness (against the asylum)

John Wieners has been described as both 'the greatest poet of emotion' (by Robert Creeley) and 'the poet laureate of gay liberation' (within the Gay Liberation press). *Solitary Pleasure* delivers us this poet raw with mid-century queer feelings. Here, we encounter a writer preoccupied with the power and magic of poetics to profoundly render love, loss and survival in the face of destruction. The poetry of Wieners – a working-class, gay/bisexual, Mad poet with femme and sometimes trans sensibilities – emerges through a radical take on Charles Olson's 'projective' poetics. A crucial element of The New American Poetry, as coined through Donald Allen's 1960 anthology of the same name and that included early writing by Wieners, Olson's dictum that "ONE PERCEPTION MUST IMMEDIATE AND DIRECTLY LEAD TO A FURTHER PERCEPTION" leads Wieners – and us, his readers – into a melange of emotions. Some of these feel and sound familiar, as the poems echo and resonate through the voices of jazz singers and starlets of Hollywood melodramas of the 1940s and 50s. 'Billie Holiday was the story / of my whole life & still is'. We're pulled into the heartstrings of a feminine glamour, that perhaps sounds campy but here is something else. Wieners revels in the 'gifts' of queer life, reading the scenes and utopian possibilities of gay subcultural, sexual spaces, often under siege from the law. He is a writer forever finding warmth around the 'small fires' of love and desire. Here, he invites us to join him, in his solitude on the page, initially (in the 50s) in the immediacy of such scenes, and later (in the 60s) in their memory. These are reflective, quiet and intimate poems, replete with flowers and tarot cards, self-deprecating turns of rhyme and phrase, and longing. Pleasure in desire lasting only ever a moment, facing heartache with a frank honesty, playing up the tragic loss of love.

John 'Jackie' (occasionally 'Jacqueline') Wieners (1934-2002) was born in Milton, Massachusetts, ten miles from Boston, the city that preoccupied his writing throughout his life. Wieners also had formative experiences living in the gay melting pot of San Francisco in the late 1950s, the era of Jack Spicer and the Beats; he spent pivotal periods of his life studying with Charles Olson at Black Mountain College in the late 50s, and in Buffalo, New York in the late 60s; and furthermore spent time as a denizen of NYC, in the company of Frank O'Hara, LeRoi Jones (Amiri Baraka) and Diane di Prima. Wieners also experienced five psychiatric incarcerations in state and private mental hospitals between 1960-1972, spending many months as an in-patient in these institutions. Over the years in Boston, Wieners found himself in dialogue with numerous poets such as Stephen Jonas, Gerrit Lansing and Edward Marshall; in the early 70s, he joined the Gay Liberation movement, in the orbit of radical gay newspaper *Fag Rag* and Good Gay Poets press in particular, and the Mental Patients' Liberation Movement, who had strong ties with Gay, Lesbian and Women's Lib. The Liberation movements challenged liberal reformist endeavours, for instance, they challenged the whole discipline of psychiatry as sexist and homophobic and shared information on the rights that mental patients had, rather than simply arguing with psychiatrists for the depathologisation of homosexuality. Wieners made poetic and practical contributions to Gay and Mental Patients' Lib, as reflected in the pages of *Fag Rag* reproduced in this volume. While sexuality and madness had long been subjects of Wieners' verse, the movements created the possibility for a radical articulation and transformation of a Gay and Mad politics that took wind in his verse from this period. Wieners spent the last three decades of his life, resident on Boston's Beacon Hill, sometimes writing and sometimes publicly reading his work.

Solitary Pleasure is an offering to readers of Wieners, old and new, selected by Richard Porter, of poems resonating tones of tenderness, queer loneliness and survival, including many texts written from the inside of psychiatric incarceration. Porter's selection reveals a humble poet, at times left with little more than his pen and emotions, verse and letters, hoping that his words will at least reach his companions in literary life and outlast the asylum walls. Drawing from the mid-1950s to early 1970s, they include classics, deep cuts, diary poems and journal entries, letters to friends, alongside newly recovered work and ephemera from university archives. The letters, such as that to Barbara Guest (16th February 1960), reveal Wieners' material situation with regard to money and incarceration, alongside his creative zeal – this particular letter musing on *Measure* (the little magazine Wieners edited between 1957-62) and enclosing a poem from *The Planets* or *Jewels*, a book or journal lost to the asylum. Other archive materials include handwritten poems, pages for *Fag Rag* featuring poems and prose from Wieners, alongside graphic illustrations, and critical writing on Wieners from Charley Shively. This includes a text not seen since its original publication, '1972-73', in which the poet reflects on the gay movement at that moment when consciousness-raising and revolt had produced new values and 'the chance to come into our own'. Wieners reflects on the receding youth movements of the time, and the challenge of an Orwellian social climate that had re-elected Richard Nixon.

Thus Wieners' writing in *Solitary Pleasure* mostly emerges from the period prior to the depathologisation of homosexuality, a time in which – in some US states – gay men, lesbians and other people who didn't conform to the strict gender roles of the period would find themselves labelled 'deviant' and 'sick', and locked up in mental hospitals. This could occur for acts as simple as public displays of affection, holding hands and kissing. Wieners had run-ins with the law on the back of public expressions of his sexuality, and episodes of involving 'delusions' (the poet's word), hearing voices, and recreational drug use led to authorities (parents and/or the police) landing the poet 'in the hospital, a total wreck, without / memory again; or worse still, behind bars'. Wieners was among one of the many homosexual and gender diverse people incarcerated in asylums during this period who faced barbaric forms of 'treatment' and conversation 'therapy' attempting to 'cure' them from their sexual and gender deviance. This included regimented and excessive use of drugs (such as Thorazine and Insulin), and Electro Convulsive Therapy (or ECT). The poet declares that his memory was destroyed by such violent "treatments", as referenced clearly in the brief lines of 'Two Years Later'. Amnesia entailed that he was unable to remember some months incarcerated in hospital in 1960-61, how he survived with the help of fellow queer writers, or that he had lost *Jewels*.

It is from these harsh conditions of survival – of the bodymind and the spirit of this queer poet – that Wieners' confronts the conditions of his existence in writing. Poetry has a critical role to play. As he writes in his pivotal 1961 poem 'The Acts of Youth':

> Do not think of the future; there is none.
> But the formula all great art is made of.
>
> Pain and suffering. Give me the strength
> to bear it, to enter those places where the
> great animals are caged.

Despite the precarity of the texts themselves, during periods of psychiatric incarceration Wieners clung steadfastly to poetry as a 'raft' or 'an actual stablizer'. Often, this writing deploys imagist verse with nouns piling up, embracing memories of love, desire and family in a pained serenity, such as in "'Now take me back to my own ruins'". In times where his deepest recesses were threated, when letters were censored and the senses controlled by medication, Wieners turned to verse, thinking of 'a million situations aided / by her manoeuvre' ("'Poetry is a desperate act'").

At the centre of *Solitary Pleasure* is Wieners' *Asylum Poems*, written inside Central Islip State Hospital (Long Island, NY) in the Summer of 1969 – the Summer of the Stonewall Riot, the uprising of drag queens and kings, Gays and Lesbians catalysed Gay Liberation. The pamphlet was published by Anne Waldman's Angel Hair Books that Fall. Wieners editor Michael Seth Stewart describes the physical object as "a large, thin book, hand-stapled, with a cover drawing by George Schneeman of a hand proffering a flower, a stylized umbel with stalks ribbing upward". It was issued in (at least) two editions by Waldman, and made a significant enough impact that a 'medical looking', anarchic bootleg of the pamphlet was also produced. Hospitalised following an arrest, Wieners describes in letters his time in Central Islip – with bleak wit – as "comparable to an extended stay in one of the worst movie houses you have ever been in". In his journal from the period, he describes that 'The patients are half-drugged. They would be / better off dead, and this kind of place / burnt off the face of the earth.' Yet, Wieners writes that he had much 'free time' to wander the fields surrounding the Asylum, to think of the 'wild fens' of Boston, and to read and fervently write. *Asylum Poems* is full of moments of such wandering and dreaming – of archetypes of handsome figures, driving fine cars naked through mountainous European landscapes – juxtaposed to the enforced solitude, bare sustenance and 'cold regulation' of the hospital. The poems at times are stark, at times eloquently embroidered in pain.

On the outside, trans people, gays and lesbians aimed bricks and blazing molotovs directly at the police, as the Liberation movements permanently altered the social and political landscape of Amerika. By 1973, Wieners was discussing in interviews how poems about "mental breakdown[s]" had "come in vogue", thanks to writers such as Anne Sexton, Sylvia Plath, Robert Lowell and Tennessee Williams. He emphasised how such writing affirmed the "hallucinatory states of unreality" (such as in Williams). Yet such writers maintained an intimate knowledge of the price of such experience and of the regimes of medication that forced order upon ones fragile senses. Wieners' writing by this time would become deeply concerned with the political and socio-economic control of poor, psychiatrised people and their embodied experiences, describing this in an often oblique and phantasmal, and sometimes direct, manner.

Solitary Pleasure continues the proposal that Wieners' writings make an offering to writers and readers of poetry, lovers, literary scholars, incarcerated people, and the rest – that memory, music and diction from the heart of struggle might blossom briefly, and that the sensation of such flowers may linger like a perfume, familiar and famous.

Nat Raha, 2023

Selected Poems

A poem for the insane

The 2nd afternoon I come
back to the women of Munch.
Models with God over

their shoulders, vampires,
the heads are down and
blood is the water-
color they use to turn on.
The story is not done.
There is one wall
left to walk. Yeah

Afterwards—Nathan
gone, big Eric busted,
Swanson down. It is
Right, the Melancholy
on the Beach. I do not
                          split

I hold on to the demon
tree, while shadows drift
around me. Until at last
there is only left the
Death Chamber. Family Reunion
in it. Rocking chairs and

who is the young man
who sneaks out thru
the black curtain, away
from the bad bed

Yeah stand now
on the new road, with the
huge mountain on your
right out of the mist

the bridge before me,
the woman waiting
with no mouth, waiting
for me to kiss it on.
I will. I will walk with
my eyes up on you for
Ever.   We step into
the kiss, 1897.
The light streams.

Melancholy carries
a red sky and our dreams
are blue boats
no one can bust or
blow out to sea.
We ride them
and Tingel-Tangel
in the afternoon.

6.20.58

A poem for painters

Our age bereft of nobility
       How can our faces show it?
I look for love.
      My lips stand out
dry and cracked with want
                of it.
             Oh it is well.
My poem shall show the need for it.

          Again we go driven by forces
     we have no control over. Only
                in the poem
    comes an image that we rule
        the line by the pen
in the painter's hand one foot
        away from me.

        Drawing the face
      and its torture.
That is why no one dares tackle it.
      Held as they are in the hands
        of forces they
     cannot understand.
             That despair
   is on my face and shall show
   in the fine lines of any man.

I had love once in the palm of my hand.
See the lines there.
        How we played
its game, are playing now
in the bounds of white and heartless fields.

Fall down on my head, love,
drench my flesh in the streams
                    of fine sprays. Like
                            French perfume
so that I light up as
                    mountain glorys
and I am showered by the scent
            of the finished line.

                    No circles
        but that two parallels do cross
And carry our souls and bodies
        together as the planets,
                Showing light on the surface
                    of our skin, knowing
                that so much of it flows through
                    the veins underneath.
                Our cheeks puffed with it.
                The pockets full.

                    2.

Pushed on by the incompletion
            of what goes before me
I hesitate before this paper
            scratching for the right words.

Paul Klee scratched for seven years
            on smoked glass, to develop
            his line, LaVigne says, look
at his face! he who has spent
            all night drawing mine.

    The sun also
rises on the rooftops, beginning
w/ violet. I begin in blue
knowing why we are cool.

3.

My middle name is Joseph and I
walk beside an ass on the way to what
Bethlehem, where a new babe is born.

Not the second hand of Yeats but
first prints on a cloudy windowpane.

America, you boil over

4.

The cauldron scalds.
Flesh is scarred.
Eyes shot.

The street aswarm with
vipers and heavy armed bandits.
There are bandages on the wounds
but blood flows unabated. The bath-
rooms are full. Oh stop up
                            the drains.
            We are run over.

5.

Let me ramble here.
yet stay within my own yardlines.
I go out of bounds
            without defense,
oh attack.

6.

At last the game is over
                        and the line lengthens.
Let us stay with what we know.

That love is my strength, that
I am overpowered by it:
                    desire
                              that too
is on the face: gone stale.
When green was the bed my love
and I laid down upon.
Such it is, heart's complaint,
You hear upon a day in June.
And I see no end in view
when summer goes, as it will,
upon the roads, like singing
companions across the land.

Go with it man, if you must,
but leave us markers on your way.

South of Mission, Seattle,
over the Sierra Mountains,
the Middle West and Michigan,
moving east again, easy
coming into Chicago and
the cattle country, calling
to each other over canyons,
careful not to be caught
at night, they are still out,
the destroyers, and down
into the South, familiar land,
lush places, blue mountains
of Carolina, into Black Mountain
and you can sleep out, or
straight across into States

I cannot think of their names.

This nation is so large, like
our hands, our love it lives
with no lover, looking only

for the beloved, back home
into the heart, New York,
New England, Vermont green
mountains, and Massachusetts
my city, Boston and the sea.
Again to smell what this calm
ocean cannot tell us. The seasons.
Only the heart remembers
and records in words
of works
we lay down for those men
who can come to them.

7.

At last. I come to the last defense.

My poems contain no
                    wilde beestes, no
lady of the lake music
of the spheres, or organ chants,

yet by these lines
I betray what little given me.

One needs no defense.

        Only the score of a man's
        struggle to stay with
        what is his own, what
        lies within him to do.

        Without which is nothing,
        for him or those who hear him
        And I come to this,
        knowing the waste, leaving

the rest up to love
and its twisted faces
my hands claw out at
only to draw back from the
blood already running there.

Oh come back, whatever heart
you have left. It is my life
you save. The poem is done.

6.18.58

A poem for the old man

God love you
  Dana my lover
lost in the horde
on this Friday night,
500 men are moving up
& down from the bath
room to the bar.
Remove this desire
from the man I love.
Who has opened
  the savagery
of the sea to me.

See to it that
his wants are filled
on California street
Bestow on him lar-
gesse that allows him
peace in his loins.

Leave him not
to the moths.
Make him out a lion
so that all who see him
hero worship his
thick chest as I did
moving my mouth
over his back bringing
our hearts to heights
I never hike over
  anymore.

Let blond hair burn
on the back of his
neck, let no ache
screw his face
up in pain, his soul
  is so hooked.
Not heroin.
Rather fix these
hundred men as his
lovers & lift him
with the enormous bale
of their desire.

Strip from him
hunger and the hungry
ones who eat in the night.
The needy & the new
found ones who would weight him down.
Weight him w/ pride and
pushing the love I put
    in his eyes.

Overflow the 500 with it
Strike them dumb,
on their knees, let them
bow down before it,
this dumb human
who has become
    my beloved
who picked me up
at 18 & put love
so that my pockets
will never be empty,
cherished as they are
against the inside flesh
    of his leg.

I occupy that space
as the boys around me
choke out desire and
drive us both back
home in the hands
    of strangers

                        6.20.58

Charles Olson   **11.24.57**
                                                              [San Francisco]

Dear Charles:

            Just to put down the random event instead of taking a
cable car.   How often
                                in fact, night before last when
you woke me up in the AM, and went to the left side of the bed
in the old bedroom on Churchill Street,
                                            she kept yelling up the stairs
for me to come down and clean house or something before Alvene
arrived, and
                    I would not, she kept insisting,
and despite embarrassment with you, a guest in the house –
            I threw a shoe
at her down the stairs on Eliot Street. It went
over her left shoulder, she shivered, like a little madonna
ringlets shaking, hands folded to her breast
she cried, but I came back in the bedroom
to talk to you said something, these things have to happen,
                                neither of us minded, you pay no. . .
            And Alvene arrived, and
                    her sister, lighter one of the two Negresses.
And off we went
the four of us
            to a narrow house on a hill.
We climbed
the wood steps, in
After of course, I introduced you to them.
                a house I never saw before.
Enuf.

1.

November 11, the holiday, I wake Rumaker, up,
we have breakfast, then walk over the back side of Nob Hill,
babbling, etc. We catch the 2 Clement Bus out Sutter Street
for Michael's taking me touring to Sutros. To the Cliff House,
                        Robin elaborated so on.
A crispe day.

After all the fooling around, the lunch and beer, our pictures
taken for a quarter, we cross to the beach
this Pacific, its sense to me of no place, no interference from
land, coming off no shore but one
                                        I have never nor will not
                            see such a girl in the surf
                            with a black jacket
                            and toreador trousers
                                        on skin tight,
                            around her head a bright red scarf
                                        4 feet long
                            so the wind takes it and is
                    the force what seems to bend her, turning on waves
                                            like a dance-er
                                except not,
                            I only remember her with her arms
                                    out, and her toe raised,
                                    foot rather, standing on one,
                        while this green Pacific longs
                        2 boys with her.
One on his elbow   and the other
full length the wet land   in blue
                                            dungarees, rolled to his
                                                    calf, by her
                                                    in the water.

                    She comes out
behind the land one's back, bends over
his face in her hands and the wind her red veil
                                up her sweater so
                        I see her arched white back,
                            not like a cat's at all, back in the water
                            she wades as we walk by.
I have to sit down and watch.
I spread an old newspaper for Mike,
I found on the bus,
and I sit on Rimbaud.
 And he looks at us once, so I have to look away.
Motions, some motion I can't set down his
head back to the street, out of the sea
                                    the young one the blonde
                    and her,

they follow him
up to the seawall, she carries their clothes.

I tell Mike I cant go away I've got to
follow them, I'll meet you up the street, wait.
And we split.
By the time I get half-way near
the 2 boys have rolled up their pants
again and are running down to the water.
The girl looks fatter
              and/
                  it's not even them.
I look at Mike smiling on the seawall. I yell
                they've gone,
                    they've disappeared.
And he says, Do you want me to tell you where –
                          loud in the wind,
                          I say No.
                I want to cross back to Playland.
        But they're probably in one of the cars.
                    Did you see them go?
        No, do you really want to look?
                We pass empty parked cars.
They went away but all the way home, when I think of them, of her
                turning on waves,
I cannot talk of how it is like
              Boston and Alan,
    what it would be like
        if I lived
      that kind of life
making
      my devotions to
      what sends it all in across the water?
Giving
      the rest up, four walls, for temple walls,
      only I know it's not like that
      on the beach, on the road,
      there is no mystery, nor God
following
      what we have known the nights, Alan and I. Balas and I
      watched the sunrise. I have sat through the night, the 3
      of them slept around me, wrote poems about it, their breath-
      ing. It was enough. Balas in the sideroom, Jan in the back-

room, Alan on the chair beside the box where I play records,
tiptoe across, fainting I will make too much noise, break the
needle, writing in the chair across the room, the sky lights
way above Boston, needing a fix, pot to sail the ship, like
those babies, if I followed them, instead of trudging up
Sutros, to the icerink, and the museum, Tom Thumb under glass
                          with the night shut out
                 the gas burner sucks up the air
where they are, will I
see them.
Like it is (what time is it) just 5 years to the minute
I get into the Studebaker with Dana and rode off into the back-
woods of Milton, never quite come out since

PS: a poem

                    to put fire in the grate, seawood
                    burn up the chimney for its night
                    ashes I will be rather than
                    settling down to just so much dust

                    in the air I cannot breathe,
                    look then to sea at Land's End
                    those roots that live on rocks, ride
                    with each surf, turning on waves.

                              John W

Deprivation

Roses, lilacs and rains
over smell of earth, freshly
turned Saturday morning for
lovers' walks down strange lanes.

Never again recaptured
never again to find, oh how
our mind rebels at this, never
again to kiss that girl

with amethyst eyes, or watch
sunrise over the harbor, never again
to visit the grape arbor of childhood,
or remove the memory stain

of these events from our firm, budding youth,
mad truth of these trysts to lose
in time their hidden passion & meaning.

Adrift a month

If I had a canoe
I'd fill it with you
then what would you do
naked and alone
to strum and shiver
under dew
of twilights quivers
handsome lord of jews
taken captive for my loins'
grotto—warmed from bondage
defended of barbarians
and kept to talent challenge —

but sit up in the night,
listen to women, wrestle, take
orders from apparitions —
better to stay within my arms.

Two years later

The hollow eyes of shock remain
Electric sockets burnt out in the
                    skull.

The beauty of men never disappears
But drives a blue car through the
                              stars.

Ancient Blue Star!

seen out the car
window.
One blinking light
how many miles away
stirs in mind
a human condition

When paved alone
created of lust
we wrestle with stone
for answer to dust.

The Waning of the Harvest Moon

No flowers now to wear at
Sunset. Autumn and the rain. Dress in
blue. For the descent. Dogs bark at
the gate. Go down daughter my soul
heavy with the memory of heaven.

It is time for famine and empty
altars. We ask your leave for by
your going we gain spring again.
No lights glimmer in the box.
I want to go out and rob a grocery store.

Hunger. My legs ache. Who will feed us.
Miles more to go. Secrets yet unread.
Dogs bark in my ears. My man lost.
My soul a jangle of lost connections.
Who will plug in the light at autumn.
When all men are alone.
Down. And further yet to go.
Words gone from my mouth.
Speechless in the tide.

How to cope with this?

A mean, dark man
was my lover
in a mean dark room
for an evening

till dawn came
we hugged and kissed
ever since, first and last
I have missed

him, his mean, dark ways.
Mean, dark days
are upon me in the sunlight
even yet, I fear his foot

feel his cock and know it
as my own, my sown
seeds to reap
when the full neap

of pleasure falls, his kiss
reminds me, our dance
in the dark, my hope
and only scope.

Queer

Do I have to accept his
repetition of rival thrust
use of assholes and bitches
to gain entry of a youth's kiss?

run by alcoholics and fakes
to penetrate each night
with the tenderness and pride
from ambition's sneer.

An Anniversary of Death

He too must with me wash his body, though
at far distant time and over endless space
take the cloth unto his loins and on his face
engage in the self same rising as I do now.

A cigarette lit upon his lips; would they were mine
and by this present moon swear his allegiance.
If he ever looks up, see the clouds and breeches
in the sky, and by the stars, lend his eyes shine.

What do I care for miles? or rows of friends lined
up in groups? blue songs, the light's bright glare.
Once he was there, now he is not; I search the empty air
the candle feeds upon, and my eyes, my heart's gone blind

to love and all he was capable of, the sweet patience
when he put his lips to places I cannot name
because they are not now the same
sun shines and larks break forth from winter branches.

Thursday, July 27 1961

To keep on writing; writing keeps
one on; on writing without a story / line,
to have nothing to say, even though
the bird song out these windows is
enough. Even though out these windows
is a world I have not despaired of
yet; and I wait to be released out
into it. And we can say the poem is
a bird song. Just that, fading in-
to silence, it lasts just as long.
Justice's song, fading into the night.

Solitary Pleasure

I wanted a companion, even a lover
to fill the empty mornings, as I knew them
on Columbus and California, but you guarded your
house too well, and the old days were over,
the old nights of jazzing around. You returned to the country alone
with your wife, and children, and I have grieved ever since.

By the seashore, in bed it was worse, days I thought it over
but nights you came back, harder then, whispering under the sheets

I see my hands getting older, and poison smoke playing over the air.
It's only memory of youth I yearn for, what I knew as a boy
the true romance of being loved, waiting for death
that never came, except when one kissed goodbye.

Pressed down by memory, I recollect hours of youth
burning brightly in evening air, how did it go, where
except now I wind up at the Plaza, with no dreams at all.

Pressed flowers fall out of a book, blue and yellow
bound together, it's better than a hotel lobby, or a
lonely tea room, buffeted out of winter snows.

It is the last day of the week, and hard-working shop girls
give thanks the weekend is here, but I have nowhere
to go, no one to see, only the old lantern on the path
to herald someone who never comes back, who has never come here.

Larkspur

then swing to Topsy, cool bass
behind the waves of
easy living
when you're in love
building up scales
like a roof
out of leaves and grass, taking a breath
on a reed your
end just right
And nowhere in sight
he says
expecting it to come down
any second
My boat
from the sky

Deepsea

5.8

Dirt under my nails,
my hands hardcaked with
abuses of lust, despair
and drugs.

Night a foreign place,
without sound or shadow
we lie abed awaiting pills
to take effect.

No poems or romance
left, only churning
without image, bereft
soft syllable denied us.

We reach, grasp for the word
as life-preserver
to sink and bob
in burning waves.

Walls alive with pictures.
faces haunt the dark. Nothing to do
but go on led by flickering of a
flame I cannot name

Stationary

I'm thinking of last evening, the feelings had
lying on the bed, dreaming of boys,
          old poets,
Bob Kaufman, seeing him on 8th Street
his hair burning out of his head.
A cigarette smoking in my hand.

A white sweater on corduroy trousers
Hearing voices of fresh lovers on the radio
next door, their spirits rush, you must
remember their kisses their soft murmurings
in the dark, like fundamental things apply
as transient storms return the centaurs.

It Was Yours

I'm a bigtime baby now
with a place all to my own
and a refrigerator light

that's always going
golden glow
when for morning's slow
I open its door for cheese and dose

oh my the clothes, the constant blows
from town and mose who bow
and close, to know this
suppose.

Cocaine

For I have seen love
and his face is choice Heart of Hearts,
a flesh of pure fire, fusing from the center
where all Motion is one.

And I have known
despair that the Face has ceased to stare
at me with the Rose of the world
but lies furled

in an artificial paradise it is Hell to get into.
If I knew you were there
I would fall upon my knees and plead to God
to deliver you in my arms once again.

But it is senseless to try.
One can only take means to reduce misery,
confuse the sensations so that this Face,
what aches in the heart and makes each new

start less close to the source of desire,
fade from the flesh that fires the night,
with dreams and infinite longing.

Loss

To live without the one you love
an empty dream never known
true happiness except as such youth

watching snow at window
listening to old music through morning.
Riding down that deserted street

by evening in a lonely cab
    past a blighted theatre
oh god yes, I missed the chance of my life

    when I gasped, when I got up and
      rushed out the room
        away from you.

Acceptance

Should I wear a shadowed eye,
grow moustaches
delineate my chin

accept spit as offering.
attach a silver earring
grease my hair

give orders to legions
of lovers to maintain manhood
scimitars away as souvenirs?

Sooush, beloved! here is my tongue.

The Acts of Youth

And with great fear I inhabit the middle of the night
What wrecks of the mind await me, what drugs
to dull the senses, what little I have left,
what more can be taken away?

The fear of travelling, of the future without hope
or buoy. I must get away from this place and see
that there is no fear without me: that it is within
unless it be some sudden act or calamity

to land me in the hospital, a total wreck, without
memory again; or worse still, behind bars. If
I could just get out of the country. Some place
where one can eat the lotus in peace.

For in this country it is terror, poverty awaits; or
am I a marked man, my life to be a lesson
or experience to those young who would trod
the same path, without God

unless he be one of justice, to wreak vengeance
on the acts committed while young under un-
due influence or circumstance. Oh I have
always seen my life as drama, patterned

after those who met with disaster or doom.
Is my mind being taken away me.
I have been over the abyss before. What
is that ringing in my ears that tells me

all is nigh, is naught but the roaring of the winter wind.
Woe to those homeless who are out on this night.
Woe to those crimes committed from which we
can walk away unharmed.

So I turn on the light
And smoke rings rise in the air.
Do not think of the future; there is none.
But the formula all great art is made of.

Pain and suffering. Give me the strength
to bear it, to enter those places where the
great animals are caged. And we can live
at peace by their side. A bride to the burden

that no god imposes but knows we have the means
to sustain its force unto the end of our days.
For that is what we are made for; for that
we are created. Until the dark hours are done.

And we rise again in the dawn.
Infinite particles of the divine sun, now
worshipped in the pitches of the night.

Reading in Bed

by evening light, at the window, where wind blows
it's not enough to wake with morning
as a child, the insistent urge of habit

sounds, to write a poem, to pore over one's past
recall ultimate orders one has since doubted
in despair. Inner reality returns

of moonlight over water at Gloucester, as
fine a harbor as the Adriatic, Charles said, before the
                                           big storm
blew up to land ancient moorings, shards against sand

of memory at midnight; ah yes the dream begins
of lips pressed against yours over waves, tides,
hour-long auto rides into dawn, when time

pounds a mystery on the beach, to no death out of reach.

January 9, 1970

ASYLUM POEMS

Asylum Poems

For My Father

1969

The Dark Brew
For Louise

At least these wounds were opened
by your love that allowed the deeper sickness in,
yea, they budded lush and festival in the dark
Silence of summer agony; when supposed love wreathed on the hill
these dark lilies grew beneath and polluted the stem

So two or three years later, I collapse under the burden,
the dark love grew immense in another's form
And silenced all holocaust in their wake.
Belladonna of morning, autumn grapes for symphony and pansy
Immediately following as birth in place of life of foetid mind
Why go on; the list is endless what these wounds
                    your love opened, fed.

First hallucination of transient loveliness; second, voices of
self-importance, guiding and cajoling, cancelling all
connection to nature; third false vision of love and
its simples; fourth murderous challenge to the
dawn of thought, and envy, jealousy, rage as
accompaniments to artistry.

Some women bathe their hands in these blossoms,
and wear them pinned to their brows, as stars; others
anoint their bodies with the petals, calling a cape of
it perfume and pay enormous prices for its
scent, pollen caught off any extreme as death
but the chaos, culmination, conflagration of
what should be love's union but is not is
simply pest of confusion in the face of order.

2.

What odor called forth by these buds, spring rain under murderous taxi tires,
a store window open to new design; the fresh arousing of debutants on
Madison Ave.?
Who knows the stop signals of their gas, their lightning roar from cliffs on
country roads,
the damp spring we allowed to forget; why stop; the abandoned goats milk
from Pennsylvania
Ah there the haven lies in some sweet vision of your collapsing purple
amethyst eyes?
within a face not mine to surmise, ring with outshooting apple blossoms
Oh, who knows the look of false surprise; the badgering pity
the dream of death lives still under morning's sunrise,
despite the clatter of broken bumper and shining festoon
of afternoon's patience for drank twilight to halo drawn's root cart.
there where I was splattered, now taken in its guise
on field and bed, as one wounded must arise
these dark bruises regard as love defended.

Espionage

I sit in the evening, not on it
this time the back porch of a building, designed in 1933,
the year when conceived, enjoying clear twilight breeze.
Finished a bottle of coke, and my last cigarette, before retiring,
a blind man stumbles out, tapping his cane loudly.

6.28.69

Suisse

Mountain'd nature is also an enemy
in that it wipes out identity.

Winters are less so
witness my chalet *au vierge*

at least maleficent are more mani-
fest before the hounds of spring

mean nothing, next to it,
the dexterous elements of spring

sound alike, bird; robin, who dunnit?
While winter comes on like a bride,

in night gown, robeing the town.
What about spring, or summer then.

Summer is a communion, don't forget it,
Be a poet to handle it.

                    The autumn lakes ablaze,
                            with brown
leaves from summer's ashes. And winter again

              Carries autumn out
its lakes gone dry, barren, fertile fields went sour

for what, the dour memory of
wheat fields' gathered harvest.

                                                6.30.69

Sustenance

Your letters and my answer
sleep in a book of poetry;

no often how plenty,
are sure company.

What anacrostic daydreams
disturb this deepest pit

searching at one time for melancholiac act;
fell victims to depression

that cheer me up. They do not stink
no instance how filled with pieties.

Verities of adolescence, proven substance
by companions through childhood,

nightmare's misery
no matter how lost, twisted and illegible

Contorted and painful truth.

Trimeters

Your lips in a cloud
the spirit that visited
before I died
still assigned to the dead

the cyanide garments
that spirit vented
with tears in payment
from provincial rent

Without personal burden
only refuge denied
such taking allowed
as federal government

6.27.69

Forthcoming

to Fernand Léger

I died in loneliness
for no one cared for me enough
to become a woman for them
that was not my only thought
and with a woman
she wanted another one

I died in loneliness
of that I am not afraid
and that I am a clank
upon the gutter, a new guard at twilight
without a dream of adolescence
frustration plucked as strong

I died in loneliness
without friends or money
they were taken off
long ago, a melodrama
sounded out my name, the glass key of a
torch song on Father's Day

I died in loneliness
away from the beach and speeding cars
back seat in love with Bunny
on the way to Howard Johnson's
beyond the blue horizon
hunting for a lost popular tune.

6.22.69

The Patio

I created eternity
to bind you within it
A scheme worthy of the pope
to keep my prince

An ivory wall, have you seen it? there
as we travel on the road, together'd
shadows flit at twilight
we will not be one of them vespers

failing in confinement.
I built it. Where are you?

6.22.69

High Noon

15 years of loving
men, women and children
with what result

Another silver Iseult
joins svelte Tristan
down a vault of tears

under what insult
account with drawn
on sorrow's bank

to sit up straight
at a stranger's voice
while he whispers miles away,

over the ocean at Cornwall
Brest, Dieppe land of melancholy
how surely these years wash away.

Gold Iseult comes to tarnish
Sylvan Tristan speeds in a white Falconetti
nude under afternoon sun

one dark haired lover on his mind
a man, not a woman inspires generations ahead
before dead legions arise

6.20.69

Private Estate

       Dancing dandelions
  and buttercups in the grass
  remind me of other summer
  flowers, simple blossoms

  roses and tiger lilies by the wall
         milk pod, sumac branches
  lilacs across the road, daises, blueberries
  snaps, cut violets

         three years ago still grow in my mind
  as peonies or planted geraniums, bachelor buttons
  in downy fields filled with clover
  lover, come again and again up fern

  path upheld as memory's perennial
  against stern hard-faced officers of imprisonment
  and cold regulation more painful than lover's arms
  or flowers charming but not more lasting.

  No, the wild tulip shall outlast the prison wall
  no matter what grows within.

                                        6.21.69

Stop Watch

          the sensation
1)   of 10 assorted dancers
          in a crowded dining room

          moving as one person
2)   in unison
          to a popular tune

          during late afternoon
3)   hip and thighs beat
          with sparkling feet

          over the stucco floor
4)   before an open door
          how fortunate, how poor

          we were without the sign,
5)   symbol of recurrence
          or occurence

          surrounded
6)   by buff walls
          it was not a waltz

          only a standard rock
7)   song, much as students
          speak in rejoinder

          to a classroom; the same decibels
8)   happened in a bookstore when I rose
          using the newspaper I had as a fan;

           the leaves of clover
9)   fluttering these three
      unities I have known

           as a tone to a bell's
10)   gong, none of them
      lasting longer

           than 10-12 seconds
11)   pressing history, light
      in memory reckoned.

                    6.20.69

Literary Reminiscence
Continued   Part 2

and the thought that a great love
affair might be awaiting still
spurs one on to imagine its
final ultimate surrender
    In the dark of the night,
under the linden branches of
a small New England academe,
to submit with one great cry
at the blind abused intrusion
of a god or king.
                To side-kick
docilely, in trust as possibly
that could be the one, whose
own experience so excited
one, there could be no choice
of course in love, before
 as Mabel Mercer
through rainy evenings, submerged

devoured memories of 21 in Back Bay
amoureuse avec la nuit, amoureux avec le printemps
en amour avec l'homme de style, speeding around

Plaza parking lots, horribly, madly, as the French might say
without means, over dreams, losing above one's means.

                          6.18.69

Morgana La Fay

The return of
again is it
love we look, not
nearly so, only

the absolute inde-
prudence of youth, in
expectation, despite
Charles Dickens.

The first time going to the museum
alone, on to the library
walking Newbury Street after
the rain, and dining out,

visiting New York City on the late evening
train. These things she thought
as the rain pelted the
trees on Long Island during the day,

and bumped into F. Scott
Fitzgerald, how he lived still
and his Long Island, always the place
to return, trembling alone

his and Zelda's Babylon
at Christmas, now living in a motel, this evocation
contained in the embrace of phantom love, and
to slip a peg, Lester Young on Times Square

6.19.69

Just an Ordinary Joe

with plain face and wrinkled forehead
superabundant in his plaints and desire,
loving one with great passion,

now on guardian's gate, forlorn, fertile
and fruitful, the little doll, how he could love
her, *so my arms ache to talk of it, the reason*

why I stay away, alone in money's prison.
The heiress' call unheard except by an impossible
man who could help her, locked interruption to

funds, social register, impotent in battle.
A true Beckett of passion brooding o'er psyche.
How to decipher their distress thus accomplish plot.

Of ancient rich girl aiding tarnished knight *en armour.*

6.30.69

Times Square

a furtive queen
hurrying across a deserted thoroughfare
at dawn.

Au Naturel

An handsome man has to think a certain way.
Honest, courageous and brave

He would be a knave
to think a different way

Another should be true, loyal and good.
He looks like he would

Come to your aid, if need be
Despite a certain look of seedy

Appearance, his disappearance would be apt
And opportune, happy

And in tune to another man's needs,
Be it pumpkin, water or seeds.

He would come to good deeds.
Of that you can be sure —
                                        Naturally.

Melancholy

Across the deep and brine
we'll go, Tristan and his lass, a ho,

up the meadow, away from men,
hand in hand, we'll lie down again.

Dark hair streaming to the wind,
Inhaling life as if our kin,

oh Tristan and his lass we'll go,
up the brine, down the glen.

Hand in hand, over men
And glad to see one another again.

sturdy lass I'll be for there,
and faint-hearted song you'll whisper.

Removed Place

When the echo falls
one will dismiss it.
When it calls again,
one will miss
it, falling in love with the present,
while one is able of it.
When the shadows enlarge, will one
enter it, or stay where
he is now.   What will one do, how

After Symonds' *Venice*

for Allen Ginsberg

Boston, sooty in memory, alive with a
thousand murky dreams of adolescence
still calls to youth; the wide streets, chimney tops over
Charles River's broad sweep to seahood buoy; the harbor
With dreams, too; *The Newport News has arrived for a week's stay*
Alan, on Summer Street sailors yet stride along summer afternoons

and the gossamer twilights on Boston Common, and Arlington Street
adrift in the mind, beside the mighty facade of convent and charnel house,
who go through those doors, up from Beacon Street, past the marooned
                                                          sunset in the

West, behind Tremont Hill's shabby haunts of artists
and the new Government Center, supplanting Scollay Square.

Who replace the all night films; and the Boston dawn
in the South End, newly washed pavements, by night's hoses.

What happens here from the windows on Columbus Avenue
to Copley Plaza, and the library, Renaissance model, the Hotel and smart
                                                          shops down

Newbury Street's lit boutique, lept by Emerson College,
who triumph light over dark, the water side
endures beside the moon and stars of Cambridge's towers

... past Park Square pavements so wide for the browser, drifters
from Northampton Street behind the Statler, by the bus stations and slum
                                                          tableaux

Finally to return to the Gardens, and the statue of George Washington
appealing to later-day shoppers to go home, in what dusk
what drunken revelling matches this reverie
of souvenirs, abandoned in the horror of public elevators

as this city is contained time, and time again the State House
from Bullfinch's pen, over School Street and Broad
          down the slope of Federal mirages over blue grass
to the waterfront; Atheneum holding all the books of men, directed
against the foe, hapless Pierre churns through the Parker House
          coming to the Vendome mentally
over the Brunswick, eternal in the mind's owl
          of phantoms stretching from boyhood.

When vows first establisht were to see this world and part
          all within it
You, Boston, were the first, as later San Francisco, and before that
New York, the South and West
penetrated, hard holds the Northwest, Chicago, Detroit
much in the same manner of industrial complexes
covering the rising cigarettes of patriots.

The Park Street Steeple as painted by Arshile Gorky zooms higher.
Slumbering city, what makes men think you sleep,
but breathe, what chants or paens needed at this end, except
you stand as first town, first bank of hopes, first envisioned paradise
by the tulips in the Public gargoyle's crotch, Haymarket
Square included spartan business enterprise and
next to South Station, the Essex evoking
          the metropolitan arena hopes entertain.

                                        August 25, 1969

Miscellaneous journal entries & ephemera

Wednesday, the 26th

What can explain the tragedy of this world? If anyone asks me why I can only write on the tragic themes, I shall surely answer, Is there any other? Has life any other theme but a tragic one? Is it only longing, pierced but the hope that cannot last. Tonight, I saw a beautiful grey-haired woman lying on a green bandana in the gutter of Tremont Street, waiting for an ambulance or death to carry her off to consolation. But the hope was there, another woman bent down as a song and fixed the bandana and seemed to stroke somehow the woman's pain. On the swaying train, coming into Park Street, a woman in a brown, soft cloth, pushing through the crushed throng with her hand to her mouth. As the door opening, she crouched, and I saw the face of a bleached blonde girl, waiting to get on, turn away, her forehead wrinkling up under the make-up. R. Greene is here, sitting outside talking about his Veronique to Gilbert. They are coming here for the week-end while I am in New York.

I hope to get to the Poetry Center while I am in the "white and glittering" city. I feeling somehow devoid of thought today. I would rather go off and read Pound's poetry in a corner, or listen to Bizet. A very sympathetic article has appeared in the Atlantic Monthly by Archibald MacLeish, titled 'The Poet as Playwright". It is devoted mainly to the criticism of T.S. Eliot's view on the theater and the use of poetry in it. Eliot feels that poetry discerned as such in the theater is a dramatic convention and that it renders to the theater-goer the illusion of the artificial. MacLeish says in effect that Eliot advocated the theory that the stage attempts to depict life as it is, rather than a new creation of life, which all art should be, we both believe.

Art has to be a new creation. It has to be like birth, that is, it has to be as striking to the onlooker as a new world is. As W.C.W repeats over and over again, in his poetry, not a copy of nature but a creation. I have had a story running over and over again in my mind concerning a man who rides the swan boats. These hold the same fixation for him as alcohol or sex would to another. His wife tries to understand. As he comes home late, she questioning, reveals, that he has been doing so well, staying away from the swans for nearly three weeks now, while the reader knows that the man is late because he had ridden the boats until nearly dark, and had only stopped because the dark had come on, and the passengers left. But that night, she finds the overlooked ticket stub in his pocket and some kind of a scene follows where all his past faults are revealed, how he couldn't hold a job because he was always late from lunch, even when he worked downtown in the shopping area, he would rush through the Common, through the contented lunchtime crowds, and plan to stay for only one ride through the lagoon but once he got on, he was unable to get off. They even had a charge account for him. The pay-check sometimes almost completely went for this. One year, he had stayed away for nearly seven weeks but one of his children had heard so much talk about the swans that he whined that he wanted to ride them. And they went. On the surface, he was calm, but the first chance he could, on the first false pretext, he fled back. After this, she left him bitterly, she sent him a card at Christmas with wild swans on it, and gloated because she knew that the lagoon was frozen and the swans caged, and the boats in dock. With the next spring, he was the first there. He got a room in the corner house on Commonwealth Avenue, so he could see them with spy glasses from his room at night. And then the little money that was left from his insurance was nearly gone, and he sold his blood, and after they refused him for safety, he turned to beggaring, and then one day without food and no shelter, his clothes in tatters about him, he ran through the park for the last time. He had snatched a woman's purse from Tremont Street and took a dollar from it, threw the contents of it into the face of three little shop-girls who were pointing at him running up the street, and then entering the gardens, very calmly, paid the man for four tickets and sat in the last row, watching the children dragging their fingers in the yellow-brown water, listened to the mothers admonishing the children dragging their long fingers in the yellow water and as the boat rounded the small ideal island in the center of his only world, with the three unsold pieces of pink paper in his hand, he slid from the boat with a small splash, just where the water came over his head.

Entry for Thursday, the 10th

I am not sure that this journal is a good idea, despite the fact that it has given me an outlet, I have not saved anything for the writing that I want to do. I read Pound, against him what can one do? If this journal were only a sideline, something that I turned to for relaxation, I would be satisfied, but it is something I turn to for expression, and that is not good.

I was very drunk last night, I was in a bar on the lower end of Washington Street in downtown Boston. I have had much to run away from, I suppose, and I did not have much money to do it with, so I smiled at hideous little people and let them buy me drinks. It is a very cheap bar, a boy they call Josie McGrath was there, and he shouted out that he was afraid to go home and shave himself because he would cut his throat. It is bottom of the barrel hangout, as a customer said, it is nowhere, and the people there have gone nowhere, and are coming from nowhere. I was pulverized, we acted up vile, I did not go out this afternoon until three or more accurately four-fifteen, and it was twenty-four exactly from where I had gone out the day before, and I had accomplished nothing, I walked the same street, I had the same clothes on except for a different pair of shorts but today, I did not have to run into a movie, today I walked along the Charles and waited for the sunset. There was none. The sun was sucked down behind great grey clouds, and left with only tiny tints on the edges of the sky.

Monday, August 17

I do not think so. I do not think that love survives man; he destroys what he has labored to build, what he has stayed awake nights over to be in the dawn, he breaks. Tear down, tear down, for all sides where he labors, he is met by fat resistance and inertia. And the challenge is to lie in its arms, and kiss it to life. To take inertia and put the electric charge in, thru sex? To meet the rock and by his body heat make lava. Let it come down what the fingers stroked. We pull down for some perverse reason. And this is not a personal destructive urge, no defense is necessary, age will calm us, make us patient, but who wants it. Why do we want the vortex of the tornado? But no questions should be asked, let us take it as we take lying in the sun. And if love does not survive, we will build another. I want a love affair, therefore I make one. I work on love as I would a canvas, or a poem, oh but that is wrong, for love takes us, I cannot stop believing it, that it takes us as the vortex does, and now when we are stopped at storm center, fatigue takes us. I will not allow old love to take me. Simply because it is old, and my blood is dried on its teeth, I will not put my head in again. I will stand outside and shake my belly so it is wrapped in the veil of myself. One finally finds after all that there is no one but the self, that this is what must be brought strong, so that its comforts are secondary, and the comfort of love shall be nothing more than a warmth in bed, and not a life to plunge the self in. There shall be no indwelling, and if this way leads to disaster, the disaster of the lonely room, there shall be no guilt, no scream of I was wrong! I should have knelt the self down, never that, no matter how dark the room, or how big the empty bed you toss on, never again the fist against the head to destroy the self. Let the other, let love die if need be, but the interior, that inner possession shall be kept at full force, and let those who want to warm their hands at it, in, let them be everywhere, but tend that fire, of the spirit.

from 'The Untitled Journal of a Would-Be Poet' (1955-56)

July 17 PM

For the poet what else is there but poems. Let the jazz
     organ pump in the afternoon. Let the dope
fiends sell their asses in the street and the disc jockeys
     spin their records, advertise wares, we are the
creators, coiners of the new
          word, line tempo
          time held to a measure. We become
what we create. Call down the entire universe into
          one syllable.

We awake to chaos & desire. It chokes
                    our throats. Puts tears
                  in our eyes. Masters of the beat, with-
held from the infidels. Dope does not replace it. The Men who
practice it our gods, our families. The mind the
                  final test. It is an
                    aristocracy. Envy for the
        titled holders of the crown. Problems. Pushed to the
                  limit each time
                we try it. Try it
                and see.
The slim books our heritage. Wise men of the world. And
                                        the way our
          mind works the way
          the poem reveals it
                self.
I can count on countless years before me with no food in my
                                        stomach,
writing out history in some dark room, doing my bit towards creating
                a new structure
                from love.
It can only be that. For any other motive we fail. And love is a
                                        sparse thing
            to nurture all
            these years.

July 22

And so now I sit alone in the house with the lights on and
Lex Baxter beating his drums
on the phonograph
The woman and the 2 children asleep on the porch
covered in blankets.
Night I think with wild cries
and a cymbal clashes somewhere in the jungle.
An uptown beat.
Tempo. Try to maintain control
of the tempo, don't fly off
like the evening star
Venus
from the sea.

How red she is
tonight
Love descends on the land. The record
ends. With
no other words but hers
in the night. Two tin cans
take over this poem. A skin
stretched over bamboo
blows out Cuban blues in the night like
Chicago. East in
the city I don't wanna go no more.
I wanta be
free as the breeze
that blows the waves
onto the shore.
Picks up speed
the tide does
with the rising of the waning/   moon.

Friday Sept 10

No thing but the song

After great pain, a formal feeling comes.
                                                          E. Dickinson

we fall back in shadows

I proceed in perverseness, be
cause there is nothing else to do
but die. And we are not allowed
that. Let others fall down be
fore us. Or being the
temple of my soul.

                              I go a—

lone serving the gods within.
            Is not art a sacrifice
            and are not we bound
                                    to it.
Sitting as "gods" on solitary thrones.
I move with pain. I wake and
wash tears down my face. Who can say
I should not walk in glory
                            when I do.
I contain my own kingdom.
            "The deific principle in nature and
            the heroic principle in man"
Move beyond that to what

            place but here
    where the poet folds his green paper
                    in the sunset and pads
            by in bare feet over the bare boards
            of this floor.

See: Marsden Hartley: *Albert Pinkham Ryder*
        The Seven Arts v.1 May 1917

308 W. 15th

The artist should not sacrifice his ideals to a landlord and a costly studio. A
rain-tight roof, frugal living, a box of colours and God's sunlight through clear
windows keep the soul attuned and the body vigorous for one's daily work.

                                                    A.P.R.

Saturday night

If I cannot have stars
in my eyes all the time,
at least let there be love.
And night sky between us.

And in the night lovers come
where there was no light before.
They bring their animal groans.
They creak the bed and cause
the dog to bark. At the moon.
I will endure this solitude.
I will rise to a new day.

There is a princess in the tower.
And steps like inside the Statue
of Liberty lead up to her.
Wooden, with grass and sunlight upon them
I would climb the stairs or stay
here in the poem

from 'The Journal of John Wieners Is To Be Called
707 Scott Street For Billie Holiday' (1959)

2.16.60

Dear Barbara Guest:

Human affairs are a matter of necessity to me this morning. The dream world being such a shambles of old cafes, florid women and liquid yellow hours. Being caught as I am right now in the grips of an asylum, there is not much I can think about but the New Measure. Will you be a part of it? Lemon cover, chocolate print or etc. This weekend (20th) I expect Irving Rosenthal + Schulman who are contacting printers and distributor, also supplying $. — Is the world too jaded for a small Tigers Eye?

Write here. c/o Dr. KORMOS. His name seems to be a "sesame" for good fortune. How I miss Washington and the Holidays. But February seems kinder to our world. Do clasp tight, even the pain. There is always laudanum. And the mechanics of the "human face". Pray for my freedom and we shall be kind enough to find release in each other's arms again.

Faithfully
John Wieners

The unconscious is a lion. He stalks. Pots from
the pool of day. Is a boy in blue riding waves.
Let the lutes play. In our tombs, jars and
narcissus sprout from the weeds. Define now.
It is not a poem. It is the paragraph. In
dent it. Mine possess no space at all.

   Crowded with the dig of his bruise. His sail
I use to bail out the boat. Rudder and mane
overflow in our concrete world. What is the wave
made of? Tides from the belly and balls of the
the bull: Aleph. See his stamp in the sky.

As we are constructed, so are the stars plotted.
The poet marks a new chart. Pinpoint pocks
the day of his birth. FDR's face makes a
new heaven. This morning astride her
precious light the hallowed woman stands
aboard.

from a bk. The PLANETS   2:/.

92

If you can forgive this intrusion of your morning, and the pressure of that; There is some need in the male psyche for possession of cool hands. We shall not expend ours. DROSTË

Wieners
Box 1A
West Harding
Massachusetts

Barbara Guest Higgins
2500 N Street
District of Columbia
Georgetown

Letter with envelope from John Wieners
to Barbara Guest Higgins, 16 February 1960

94

Letter from John Wieners to Robert Wilson
of Phoenix Book Shop, 4 October 1964

95

October 4, 1964

Dear Bob:

    I am writing you a funny, sad letter. I wonder
if you could advance me $25.00 on royalties (I am
writing the same letter to Jim Carr) as my sister
is expecting a box spring on Wednesday, for which
she gave me the money, $67.07, part of which I spent.
It is coming C.O.D and I only have $40.00. Will you
do this, and send me the money so I will have it
Wednesday, otherwise the box-spring goes back, and I
am held in dishonor in the house. This is very im-
portant to me, and I will not bother you again this
way, I just went over my head, and bought my friends
in Chinatown a big dinner, and now I have no money
to pay for this Beautyrest; it is coming, but they
don't know it is C.OD. It will be allright, if I
have the money to meet the man at the door. I know
this is unfortunate, and I will not get into this
mess, again. Please be a good boy and do this for
me. I think I will be able to pay you back on royalties,
if the book sells. Which it will, given a little time.

    Can you let me know right away, otherwise, I will
have to go out and steal, pass bad checks, and maybe
land up in jail. All of which, I do not want to do.

                  Love,

                  John

The other money will go to my mother's charge account,
on which I owe $30, for beauty preparations.

Holy

Silence, holy unmoving mouths
of my beloveds, holy faces shining
in the night, holy light.

Holy plane flying in the stars
Holy moon rising, holy sun setting
Hole of the planets between which

Nothing lives. Holy death. This last
The hardest to bear. Holy friends gone there.
Holy songs haloing their heads lost to sight.

Last Entry

My mind is coming back slowly, I can tell. The inner
voices make sense now. They no longer tell me to do ir-
relevant things or contradict each other.

    I like writing better with a free-flowing pen.
Its spirit seems to run freer and with more spirit.

Of course, when one pain decreases, another increases.
Now the pain in my head increases, from sinus.
It is concentrated mainly over the right eye.
    How good it is to talk again and make sense.

The mind is a structure that can be blasted a-
part, into a thousand bits, all of them not making
sense except in isolated fragments, though brilliant
                    still frustrating to the creative mind which
      is trying
                  to communicate itself in sentences more
      complex
            than statements of help or longing or dismay.

           no inter-relationship at all, it is
the mind's job
how to build that relation back, call it sanity
When it coheres, when these fragments congeal, when there is
  a memory or past, when
the structure holds, when a sentence can be
more than a beginning and an end, one can take a chance and
          leap out, not compulsively as before, but with more
surety, when there is rhyme in the mind's question
      not confusion or chaos, the
         handwriting holds, unless
            one wants it to go (it springs
              from reading, I think)
          and talking with friends, wise men, gods, saints,
  poets, ah yes not egos
when one is sure of himself, not interrupted by a thousand
contradictions or possibilities; one can make style out of
    himself when one is led not by distraction

however compulsive that may be. The
rest is silence. And frightening to be hold in a writer.

Ah well,
the frenzy ~~on this page, it takes to~~ it takes to communicate a
~~belief knowledge~~
            that thought.

                    Love,
                John Wieners
            November 28, 1965
                4AM — Sunday
                    Morning

from BLAAUWILDEBEESTEFONTEIN (1965)

Recipe for 'John Wieners' Orgasm Tonic'
Fuck You: a magazine of the arts, Number 5, Volume 9, July 1965

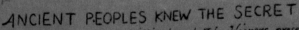

ANCIENT PEOPLES KNEW THE SECRET

Now, in our time, the brilliant poet John Wieners presents

JOHN WIENERS'  **ORGASM TONIC**

MEN! DO YOU want

- a smooth rippling ultra-tense glans?
- longer life to your hardon?
- a dick a chick's proud to cop?
- a cock-head tough as a cue ball?
- daily spurt scenes?

DRINK UP!!

a spoonful ✕ per day

Says John Wieners: "It's absolutely guaranteed.
I bathe in buckets of sperm because of it."

bottled & freaked
by the FUCK YOU/ products corp.
at a secret laboratory
somewhere in the Lower East Side
New York City, USA.

A four ounce bottle, only $1.50, from your dealer.

FUCK YOU/ A MAGAZINE OF THE ARTS. Number 5, Volume 9, July, 1965.
Printed, published, edited by Ed Sanders at a secret location in the
lower east side, New York City.
NOTES ON CONTRIBUTORS:

PINDAR/ was a wonderful 5th century Theban poet & eagle-freak.
JOE BRAINARD/ is a young genius artist who freaks his work out of
N.Y.'s Alan Gallery. Mr. Brainard's new novel is EAGLE-QUEEN, based
on the life of Pindar.
TOM VEITCH/ is an associate editor at TIME Inc. His acerbic witticisms
are more often edited out of his Time texts but not until hysterical
prostatic cackle rounds have been made thru the senior editors'
offices. His is the author of LITERARY DAYS, a book of reminiscences,
published by Ted Berrigan's C Press.
HARRY FAINLIGHT/ has dragged his prolapsed rectum off Times Square
back to London   to scarf up some international rubber pants
trade. His books of poetry include the legendary A DICK SPENTO, & the
recent LONDON, A BOOK OF POEMS. Freak them up!
--notes on contributors cont inside page--

Now take me back to my own ruins, the raft
on the Neponset in February, with Mother
beating thru the woods, red coat and all
autumns come down, leaves caught in flood.

Gutters, Michael Murphy raking blue smoke
by the old stone wall, swinging off birches,
beechnut, the big rock and hot tin barrel.

Roll me over one more time, Marion for
this scorch in the sun, Sister who haunts me
in alleys off Blue Hill Avenue.

Rats under the crib, smashed glass and
blankets hung out all windows of this mustard

seed world.

MISSED LUNCHEON

1)

Such sterile unconsidered order to avoid as stale bread
Better to write and work at decipherment of one's
Personal ego; submerged most of the day by the
                              world in ceaseless movement
Afloat only in madness, doubtful, that is mainly mal-
                    nutrition

Since one meal less offsets satiety; wonder
not at outcome: a tryst beneath trees
                              closes
the book climaxed on that freshness, returns moisture to
                              the cheeks,

rose to the lips, dilated eyes color of si
                    depth, aban
      society, respect, moral law an

   Empyrean blue cloud

      As delicate an   *page torn*

shuffled out of order; writing poetry
                                        delectable
trance in opposition held at such
                              wonder.
One may not indulge too frequently for fear
the borean depths engulf, flood lost.

Doubtful reason aided sense; indiscriminate
                              course to hold

Memory firm, a place enlodged
                        embedded, entwined

variously; walking, riding hypnotized on
                                    trains,
drugged, visiting the sick, staying
                              close to one's family.

Some means to take towards erection of sightly edifice,

In place of fried chicken and french potatoes,
                        delicious to behold, electrified.

"Best to spit out that plum."

The last line of 4th stanza & final one
Title of *2nd work in third poem*

July 6th 1969
State Hospital

Memory

It's fabulous to fly at this hour as heavy
whales through a deep sea; flying fish in grace

and harmony to that pure instant of crystal beauty
Pater speaks of, without being burned in
immolation to that *instant.*

Poetry is a desperate act,
the last-minute decision
against self-annihilation,

life a shedding of
embittered circumstance,
but poetry has done so much

in terms of superficial grace,
a million situations aided
by her manoeuvre.

New friends made, bad companions
left behind; even violence offended
through her charm.

And we the benefactors –
these trying moments will pass, but poetry

endures, her profit as a glass to count time.

Is it truth what they say in despair.

It's one thing I have held to,
over the years, as one's parents
in a seeding ground. Not penny ante

but an actual stabilizer to hold to,
then they won't let you out, in a
rainstorm or otherwise. How I would
love to

be kept at home! away from this madhouse.
But I have to wait. One has to be patient.
It may take even years to get out of here,

but I live as if I were going tomorrow. And
                              each thought
directed toward makes more nervous than I
                              ought to be, She said,

you'll be out by Thanksgiving and god I honestly
wish it. That's not years, that's not even
months, that's only of course the week after
Labor Day; that's only somebody's vacation.

Uncle Cyril meanders in his mind from a steel
                              walker
the streets of morning for just one more instance
                              of normality
in a black suit, tie and Homburg. I might be him
And Ed Sanders my beacon from Atlantis

paltry, corrupt and undeniable.

Doggerel

Alone in an afternoon's
misery, but not so compromised
as unable to compose, unable

to wander the fields, the lanes

the sunlight wanders on the
windowsill. The dial on the radio,
the man closing a car door, or

running water in the room next door.

No elation, only this effort
to combat nervous anxiety.
Some might call it heroic:

when I have memories of other afternoons,
they do not last, nor shall this one.

on the market, it's dead sperm in the back of
                    the brain, that brings such pain––

give me a libertine's arches any day.

                Waiting only for supper.
                                In ten years time,
I will be waiting for supper even then,
and my publishing output have doubled.
Forty-five is still young enough for
                                adventure and
                        romance.
Might even return to San Francisco for a
                    round the world trip,

                                        i.e. if still
        living and I still want to be desperately.

        Not wasting time but clear
                        headed,

they come at such long intervals, these seconds
                of clear headedness.

this book is a gift from a boy with a house above
                                    a harbor.
A pink pavilion set apart from the anger and
                          stress of the sea,
crashing perennially to the sands below,

There was loveliness once and I want to know
where it's gone. In the memory of it, it lives.

But as now only recollected, where as before it
                    was immediately experienced.
These do not sound like sick things to dwell on.

But the nervous pain in limbs as arthritis
or crippling of sensory powers through the
medicine I'm under causes anxious panic.

            A bad day to go through again.
            Once perhaps I will even look back

on this time, fondly, but I hope it is a
happy time that provokes, and not more
lonely than this one. Gingerly, is the word.

I would use on this experience,

            Of course in another place
            I could get up and dance
            the spirits away. I cannot

do that here. I am a slave
in misery here, watching
things I do not care for.
Pool tables, crap games,
swearing and cursing
myself in antagonism
with everything.

Dear girl, tell me how this sun shines,
give me a secret for today, tell me
what happens beforehand, whether
I will be happy or sad.

Do I know you well enough
to go on with this, in my sickness
and health? a modicum of each
is enough for what I want is

someone else. A true love to own
and keep. To sleep next to,
                          it's been
so long since I've had anyone to
share my lonely whirlwind with

            on a darkling night,
            as speed races by in high
            motored sports cars.

Tell me, dear girl, why I am
                this way

from 'A New Book From Rome' (1969-1970)

in memoriam

Prescott Townsend at the
testimonial given in his
honor Saturday, April 7,
1973, at the Charles Street
Meeting House, a month
before his death.

PRESCOTT TOWNSEND

1894---1973

On the evening of Saturday, April 7,
1973, members of the activist gay commu-
nity sponsored a program at the Charles
Street Meeting House to honor Prescott
Townsend, Boston's venerable citizen ex-
traordinaire and most senior gay libera-
tionist.

Organized on short notice, between 30
and 40 people attended the affair. Prescott
was presented as "The World's Oldest
Practising Homosexual," an introduction
which made Townsend smile. Truth be told,
Prescott was seen in the company of a
youth only days before, in which, let us
hopefully assume, there was intimacy.

The tribute was comprised of a short
biography of P. T., anecdotes related by
friends, and the presentation of flowers
and fresh fruit. Following this, An Early
Clue to the New Direction was shown. It is
a mid-1960's film done by Andy Meyer in
which Prescott is featured. Part of his
performance is given over to detailing his
much celebrated Snowflake Theory of Sex-
uality.

After the tribute, Prescott attended a
party.

As it happened, this was P. T.'s last
public appearance.

Prescott Townsend died May 18, 1973,
in his Garden Street apartment on Beacon
Hill. He was 78. It appears to have been
a case of his having chosen to die, since
one source reports that P. T. had refused
food and medication for his last few days.

His body was cremated.

An elaborate service was held in his
memory at the Arlington Street Church of
which Townsend had long been a member.
Lacking publicity, few turned out for the
service. Several relatives and a few
friends of long acquaintance were there.
Prescott, who had literally known thou-
sands of people in his many years, was
commemorated by just a handful.

But he is remembered. His death
leaves a vacuum not only within the gay
community but within Boston at large.

Beside being an early gay advocate and
proselytizer, Prescott was of that Boston
breed of hearty Yankee Individualists for
whom fighting injustice was almost second
nature.

It was Prescott's wish to have his ashes
interred in the Old Granary cemetery be-
hind Park Street Church where his ances-
tors, up until 1812, were buried.

oston, Mass.   Summer, 1973

FAG
RAG
FIVE

50¢

Christopher Isherwood:
An Interview

Allen Young:
On the Death of Marshall Bloom

Group Sex

John Wieners

Everyone is ready for a poet of opium and drugs. (After all, Confessions of an Opium Eater is a perennial favorite.) Insanity is also quite in style; some peoples have even made their visionaries shamans. Robert Lowell is always teetering at the brink. John Berryman jumped over to the other side. Suicide, insanity, despair, drugs--La sottise, l'erreur, le peche, la lesine--these are the lifeblood of "modern" poesy.

But cocksucking? People (especially menpeople) are not so comfortable about The Poet As Pervert. Rimbaud, Verlaine, Whitman, Lorca, Shakespeare, etc., notwithstanding, there are several ways of trivializing the faggot-poet's soul when his existence is too strong to be denied.

You can say: Oh, how cute! Our favorite perversion--John Wieners. As though cocksucking were a phenomenon so far removed from YOU that you are only an observer, an historian, like reading in college about the Trojan War (as opposed to Homer, not to mention Sappho).

Or you can say: How noble! He creates beauty out of such a dung heap of hideous sorrow and malignancy. Who'd ever think anyone could find beauty and love in such sordid material? But, thank god, he's lifted himself out of that sickening world with his poetry. Now we can teach him at Harvard!

Or you can say: His sexual life is insignificant. It's his poetry that counts! What he does in bed is not important. He's a MAN, a great POET; forget all that faggot queer stuff. He's respectable enough. Don't mention that awful private life he leads--it's in bad taste to talk about such things.

All this is high comedy to me as a fellow faggot/poet. If you say I'm a faggot in a poem, out comes pontifical Norman Podhoretz in his black leather boots, jacket and chains to say (as he did about Ginsberg) that you're an exhibitionist, you can't be a poet. Or you can hide in your closet like W. H. Auden, write "porno" poems and save your eternal thoughts for the church, collected works and prize committees.

John Wieners bypasses all this and brings gayness out so that no one can dismiss it. He's simply followed the advice of such great poets as Williams/Pound/Olson & Co. First of all, report exactly what you find at hand, what you actually see, your world. ("I would be an historian as Herodotus was, looking for oneself for the evidence of what is said..." Letter 23). Secondly, report it in your own voice, your own language, your own song.

John travels right off from his world of cocksucking, gay bars, Greta Garbo, johns, bushes, lovers, Judy Garland records, Mae West, Billie Holiday, Marilyn Monroe, and from himself into his poetry. ("A poem is energy transferred from where the poet got it. He will have several causations, by the way of the poem itself to, all the way over to, the reader." sd. Olson.)

One can no more dismiss the gay part of John's poetry by saying it's insignificant than dismiss Gloucester by saying it's only a minor artifact in the Maximus Poems. As an exercise, one could scan all the Olson commentary (now becoming nearly as monumental as the man himself) and substitute "cocksucking" for "Gloucester." Or go to the beginning of this article and substitute "Gloucester/Olson" for "cocksucking/Wieners."

You get the idea. The quality is different. People can accept Gloucester without BLOCKADES to understanding, except for its being there. (The only danger in Gloucester is that "students" will become archaeologists of Cape Ann trivia instead of morning.)

I would sing C. Olson's "The Lordly and Isolate Satyrs" to John Wieners and the gay Carnival crowd as Olson sang it to his motorcycle club:

THE WILD TULIP SHALL OUTLAST THE PRISON WALL

by Charley Shively

Hail them and watch out. The rest of us,
on the beach as we had previously known it, did not know
there was this left side. As they came riding in from the sea
--we did not notice them until they were already creating
the beach we had known was there--but we assume
they came in from the sea. We assume that. We don't know.

In any case the whole sea was now a hemisphere,
and our eyes like half a fly's, we saw twice as much. Everything opened, even if the newcomers just sat, didn't
for an instant, pay us any attention. We were as we had been,
in that respect. We were as usual, the children were being fed pop
on a beach. Something had happened but the change
wasn't at all evident. A few drops of rain
would have made more of a disturbance.

We look at them and begin to know. We begin to see
who they are. We see why they are satyrs, and why one half
of the beach was unknown to us. And now that it is known,
now that the beach goes all the way to the headland we thought
we were huddling ourselves up against, it turns out it is the
same. It is beach. The Visitors--Resters--who, by being there,
made manifest what we had not known--that the beach fronted wholly
to the sea--have only done that, completed the beach.

                                        The difference is
we are more on it.

Among the readers of John's poetry, only the gay have really responded to the whole beach, the left side as well as the right; most people (particularly straight men) keep huddled up against the headland, protecting their eyes, hiding their flys, their mouths from the lordly and isolate satyrs; everything remains closed as a generation and nation of uptight asses (including a lot of poets) continue sucking their pop bottles & nibbling potato chips.

A great part of that gay world includes a very crunchy system of values sometimes called "Camp," which few if any straight white males ever get through, particularly the Olson/Williams/Pound crowd. They are all so utterly deadly serious--pontifical and portentous, metaphysical and masculine. One catches this in Olson's grudging admiration for Hart Crane (who was only a poet of "nominatives" to them, that is word embroidery, not of fucking verbs like men should be). And John Wieners, although vastly changed by hearing Olson read during Hurricane Hazel, September 11, 1954, pushes into country beyond Olson's reach. He travels into that land of pink peanuts and orange ladies of Frank O'Hara and other good gay poets.

(continued on page 14)

The Loneliness

It is so sad
It is so lonely
I felt younger after doing him,
and when I looked in the mirror
my hair was rumpled.

I smoothed it
and rooted for someone else
or wanted to satisfy myself,
Almost seven,
No hope left.

How can a man have pride
without a wife.

I spit him out on the floor.
Immensely relieved
After ejaculating
Imagining myself up my lover's ass
he coming by himself.

Looking out the window, for no reason
except to soothe myself
I shall go to the bookstore
And pretend nothing happened.
Enormously gratified.

Feeling like a girl
stinking beneath my clothes.

                    --John Wieners

mentalia cognition
      & mercedes ignition

        blood sisters in silver
         -trimmed velvet

red hung with families
    of toothy bottom-up bats
tiny skilled claws
leave red retching--
    mercedes hissing
    soft mercy cries

mentalia in saturnine plated threads

     advances to amaranth
retreats in blue
    smoulders at length
    behind smoky green haze

black pupils black depths
calculating the time to arise
    to an early toilette
    to bare his legs
    but not his dark face
shoulders drifting in silky black waves
    lost in lathered coral

strength learning mystery
knows rouge proves true

    sweet lips compress soft
     passion almost sneers
    and moans pretty to warm

mercedes of metal-flake
lashes and heels
    encircling the street
    in chic tones and sparks

    cat bodies delight in veils
not sight

    velvet come to me mercy
    your pretty boy blonde

ruby sharp kiss me now slivers

        --Diedre Phelps

1972-73, now that drugs and their addicts' debris have left the scene, a new purity has hit life after dark. No more all-night rooting in the garbage. The parks are clear and the music cabarets are clean. Strangely enough this decade, it seems that the avant-garde homophiles; before in the 50's and 60's there was never such a thing, except in isolated cases, have adopted exemplar mores.

Gays sprout beards, around the vulva of a mouth, this can be quite exciting, and it also makes appear that effeminists are more manly. Their garb is rough. You can't tell a straight from a lady, and cruising promenades teem to capacity with the style and accoutrement of the far-out renegade and cool beat. These attitudes were to the exception and in the minority after sundown in the late 50's.

It seems a period of new experimentation and confidence and excitement has broken on the shore of our sexual "minority." Guitars get the attention of the male torso, and with the unleashing of an unconscious that the so-called "sexual deviate" inherits, and which by nature has been subjugated for three thousand years, who knows the telling where it may lead to.

Boys now dress in the clothes of their male idols, making them stand up to any butch competition. Homophile movements grow strong and proliferate weekly, without any advertisement, some out of a common need.

Drugs were dangerous. They leveled the ranks of the post-beat generation, some it was pointed out dispensed by fascist doctors to decimate the young. Terrorizing and terrified bands of youth swept over the boulevard and through the ghetto areas of New York, San Francisco and Boston.

Now that seems mainly over. We have survived, Simon and Garfunkel, and Allen Ginsberg and Fidel Castro. That seems good and we welcome the chance to come into our own, to take our place, as adults, politically potential, and emotionally capable, if not this decade perhaps after Orwellian 1984 ends, and the American Revolution leaves us unvanquished, able to take our place as victor and heroes, beside our competent, newly-trained lovers.

        --John Wieners

After the Orgasm

Aw, what is fame, is it
worth it, that people should know your name
when you have a loveless shame

the taxi-driver last night, "Do we have a celebrity
with us?" and the only thing that helps
is to think of the others who haven't made it.

At least at this time. We sit around behind
grey window frames, and when it comes,
we'll know we worked hard for it

every priceless moment. Now listening to torch songs,
we dream of those revered days,
as if we haven't enough of it now

when our flesh shall be old,
and the young bodies shall mean the universe for us,
only to find it's some worthless punk who ends up in your arms.

--John Wieners

(continued from page 11)

John's position here vis-a-vis the Olsonians emerges clearly in a short piece called WOMAN, which he did in the series "A CURRICULUM OF THE SOUL." This curriculum-pamphlet series comes from an outline of Olson's for a curriculum of the soul. Various poets have each taken a word from the outline (talk about nominatives!) and written a pamphlet. In the list of available and projected word/works, there is not a single woman author; the whole curriculum is to be run by men. But the word/world "woman" was in Olson's outline, so they gave it to the most obvious faggot, the one who wrote "a poem for cock-suckers."

Let the fag do the dishes when there's no woman in the house.

So, John "Working without guidelines here, I abjectly suspicion retrograde aspersions as to why I do not accept this Assignment as an insult...," but he doesn't; the anima of Frank O'Hara hovers over the work. "Frank O'Hara could not attend. Even I had to borrow a $1000, still unpaid, to reach the Festival." It's Camp-town time in the valley & John lays it on for the dullards sucking their pop bottles on the other side of the beach; and more seriously conspires "alone to return glamor and excitement out of the tedium, apparent in some monotonous tasks, they /women, we/ must undertake."

And the illuminated satyr lordly and isolate in his assignment takes it into the streets: "in closing I announce Rose Kennedy and Jacqueline Onassis as tantamount heroines to survive the dinginess of ugly politicians who drink and brawl at others' expenses." John did not just write, render trivial his world. On April Fool's Day, 1971, shortly after finishing WOMAN, he became Rose Kennedy/ was Rose Kennedy: a play on words few Olsonian lines can become. He was swiftly arrested at Boston's Logan Airport by "the dinginess of politicians" and imprisoned for several months until he could convince the "national leadership, stretching out of D.C. to B.C.," that he was a man, that he was only joking, that he could be trusted to "pass" into the men's world. His Selected Poems came off the press while he was still incarcerated in the Taunton State Hospital.

What the airport, the police, the doctors and so much of the world abjures and cannot stand is any form of feminine identification in men (or in women really; there are few places for a "woman identified woman," even fewer for a "woman identified man"). That is why many men find John's poetry "difficult"; they can't comprehend this feminine sensibility.

The woman identification has many parts. For instance in music, John's imagination has always been fueled by women blues singers: Judy Garland and Billie Holiday of course, but also less well knowns like Ruth Etting, Helen Morgan, Mildred Bailey, Carmen McRae, Dakota Station and a host of others. His sensibility follows their perceptions with echoes and bits of their songs throughout his poetry.

And among schoolday poets, Edna Millay came first followed by Emily Dickinson and H.D. He was weaned as a poet on women's verses, not Vachel Lindsay, T.S. Eliot, or Ezra Pound or any other among the tromping troubadors.

Finally, we have the movie stars: Greta Garbo, Marilyn Monroe, Marlene Dietrich, Lana Turner and Elizabeth Taylor to name a few.

John must have read every movie magazine (and there are millions) ever published, lingering on the curious gossip and lingerie of Hollywood like a buggy eyed teenage lover. Yet he sees more in the movies than might be immediately transparent. He has off and on through the years written his unique movie reviews and commentaries. For instance, April 1, 1962 in FLOATING BEAR: in a "Dear Billy," letter John writes, "Elizabeth Taylor farted incessantly during the Paris premiere of LAWRENCE OF ARABIA, creating such a stench that Richard Burton, her escort, often was obliged to hold his nose. This gave some members of the audience (seated beyond Miss Taylor's immediate vicinity) the impression that Burton disliked the picture. His actual opinion isn't known, but when they asked Liz how she had enjoyed herself, she replied, 'There was a lovely sunset at the end, and I think there was one at the beginning, too.'" This is more than burlesque Louella Parsons; it reveals John at the heart of his material, while all the time hovering over it, distanced, floating beyond the turnips in their loamy soil.

From Susan Sontag we should all know about "Camp," and through Andy Warhol be familiar with its vagaries. John was close to this experience. Gerry Malanga, sometime Warhol ex-superstar, for instance, did the cover and illustration for his book Nerves. And there are similarities in Wieners' and Warhol's utilizations of movie stars, singers and fan magazines. But the differences between the two are more than the differences between a plastic artist and a poet.

Besides being slightly pasty and solemn, Warhol has been caught up in the mass media network he had evidently sought to exploit (ah, the hunter & hunted joined?). In a new underground magazine called MANIFEST DESTINY, John recently wrote about Warhol. "You've got to hand it to the master charlatan of a decade ago. He's got yearning Beverly Hillbillies' avant-garde eating out of his yard... What is sold's a cheap capitalization of mass-media and inherited truth without even stereotyped attention from genius." This "attention" makes all the necessary difference between being "cute," chic or fashionable and being a poet. ATTENTION is key here, a basic-- it doesn't mean solemnity but it does mean CARE, care as caritas and care as caution and care as watching. Attencion!

John brings a light purity, passion and love out of "Camp" sensibility. He loves his material even as he reweaves it, and without that love you have no soul. "Morgana La Fay" from Nerves is a fine example:

The return of
again is it
love we look, not
nearly so, only

the absolute inde-
prudence of youth, in
expectation, despite
Charles Dickens.

The first time going to the museum
alone, on to the library
walking Newbury Street after
the rain, and dining out,

visiting New York City on the late evening
trains. These things she thought
as the rain pelted the
trees on Long Island during the day,

and bumped into F. Scott
Fitzgerald, how he lives still
and his Long Island, always the place
to return, trembling alone

his and Zelda's Babylon
at Christmas, now living in a motel, this
                              evocation
contained in the embrace of phantom love,
                              and
to slip a peg, Lester Young by Times
                              Square

Finally and obviously the immense quality of love (care) in John's commitment to people, life, the world, everything around him is everywhere evident, as in "Morgana La Fay." Although I see nothing wrong in despair, I see John as a poet of despair. In a FUCK YOU anthology on despair, Harry Fainlight wrote, "The despair market is already cornered/ Wieners has got it sewn up tight as.../"

But the subjects John treats that might seem desperate to the straight audience, mass media, university don or suburban family poet are not maudlin when rendered into poetry by John Wieners. His objects are not objects of pity or onus to either himself or his audience. They are not subjective objects, personal misfortunes (as say in Denise Levertov's anti-war poems); they are objects of poetry/eternity.

No, the wild tulip shall outlast the
                              prison wall
no matter what grows within.

excerpts of contributions by John Wieners to Issue 5 of *Fag Rag*
a gay liberation newspaper published in Boston, MA (1973)

November 24

Dearest Johnnie:

Your charity and courtesy remain
in the face of travail. Other poets stretch
out their arms to you before the dais of
eternity, where your esteemed creation
takes its place for our short years.

Allen shall revere your poems for
testament to audiences, we shall create
by our fervor through more sacred
decades, by your person. We have
served poetry and men. That dedication
shall keep the fire of your body bright
before my eyes.

I have always regarded you as an

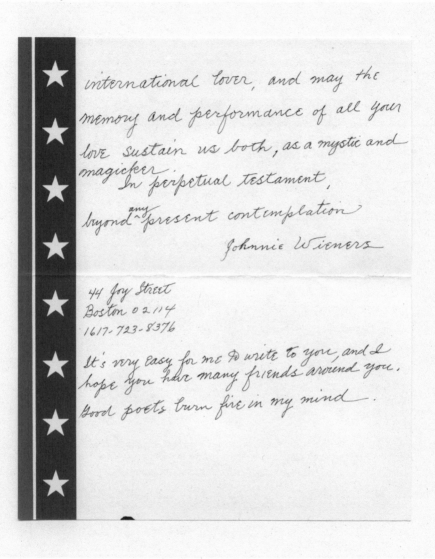

international lover, and may the memory and performance of all your love sustain us both, as a mystic and magicker.

In perpetual testament, beyond any present contemplation

Johnnie Wieners

44 Joy Street
Boston 02114
1 617-723-8376

It's very easy for me to write to you, and I hope you have many friends around you. Good poets burn fire in my mind.

Letter to John Giorno from John Wieners (undated)
courtesy John Giorno Foundation

SUPPLICATION

O poetry, visit this house often,
imbue my life with successes,
leave me not alone,
give me a wife and a home.

Take this curse off
of early death and drugs,
make me a friend among peers,
lend me love, and timeliness.

Return me to the men who teach
and above all, cure the
hurts of wanting the impossible
through this suspended vacuum.

from 'Early Morning Exercises' (mixed media and collage on paper, 1985)
by Francesco Clemente and John Wieners
courtesy Studio Francesco Clemente

John Wieners in City Lights Bookshop, San Francisco c. 1984
Photograph by Raymond Foye

Editor's note

Thank you to Raymond Foye, Michael Seth Stewart, Robert Dewhurst and Nat Raha for your invaluable kindness, generosity and guidance in compiling this collection.

For help with research, my thanks to Bonnie Whitehouse at John Giorno Foundation, Tim Murray at the Morris Library, University of Delaware, Yana Rovner at Studio Francesco Clemente and to the friendly person on the front desk of the National Poetry Library, who pointed me in the right direction on that first day.

And, of course, a very big thank you to all the editors of previous publications featuring Wieners's work, in which many of the poems, letters and journal entries included in these pages were first published: David Haselwood (*The Hotel Wentley Poems*), James F. Carr and Robert A. Wilson (*Ace of Pentacles*), Anne Waldman and Lewis Warsh (*Asylum Poems*), Tom Maschler (*Nerves*), Raymond Foye (*Selected Poems: 1958-1984 and Cultural Affairs in Boston, Poetry & Prose 1956-1985*), Patricia Scanlan (*Strictly Illegal*), Michael Seth Stewart (*Stars Seen in Person: Selected Journals of John Wieners*), James Dunn (*A New Book from Rome*), Robert Dewhurst, CA Conrad and Joshua Beckman (*Supplication*), Ed Sanders (*Fuck You! A Magazine of the Arts*) and Charles Shively and the editorial collective of *Fag Rag*.

Finally, my thanks to the Republic of Consciousness Prize 2023 for awarding me a grant that paid for a new computer in the nick of time, and to Charlie Porter and Orpheus, for more than I can say.

Selected Bibliography

Books, Pamphlets and Chapbooks

The Hotel Wentley Poems, San Francisco, Auerhahn Press, 1958, revised edition, San Francisco, Dave Haselwood

Ace of Pentacles, New York, James F. Carr and Robert A. Wilson, 1964

Asylum Poems, New York, Angel Hair Books, 1969

Nerves, London, Cape Goliard Press, 1970

Selected Poems, London, Jonathan Cape, 1972

Behind the State Capitol: Or Cincinnati Pike, Boston, The Good Gay Poets, 1975

Selected Poems: 1958–1984, ed. Raymond Foye, Santa Barbara, Black Sparrow, 1986

Cultural Affairs in Boston, Poetry & Prose 1956-1985, ed. Raymond Foye, Santa Rosa, Black Sparrow, 1988

Strictly Illegal, Patricia Hope Scanlan and Jeremy Reed, Yapton, West Sussex, Artery Editions, 2011

Journals

The Journal of John Wieners is to be called 707 Scott Street for Billie Holiday 1959, Los Angeles, Sun & Moon Press, 1996

A New Book from Rome, ed. James Dunn, Lowell, MA, Bootstrap Press, 2010

Stars Seen in Person: Selected Journals of John Wieners, ed. Michael Seth Stewart, San Francisco, City Lights, 2015

Yours Presently: Selected Letters of John Wieners, ed. Michael Seth Stewart, Albuquerque, University of New Mexico Press, 2020

PhD Theses

"For The Voices": The Letters of John Wieners, Michael Seth Stewart, New York, The City University of New York, 2014

Ungrateful City: The Collected Poems of John Wieners, 2 vols. Robert Stuart Dewhurst, University of Buffalo, State University of New York, 2014

Queer Capital: Marxism in Queer Theory and Post-1950 Poetics, Nat Raha, Falmer, University of Sussex, 2018

Published in the U.K. by Pilot Press

Edited by Richard Porter
Introduction by Nat Raha
Cover photograph by Leni Sinclair

ISBN 978-1-7397029-7-7

Printed on 100% recycled paper